GRADE 2 VOCABULARY

Fun-filled Activities

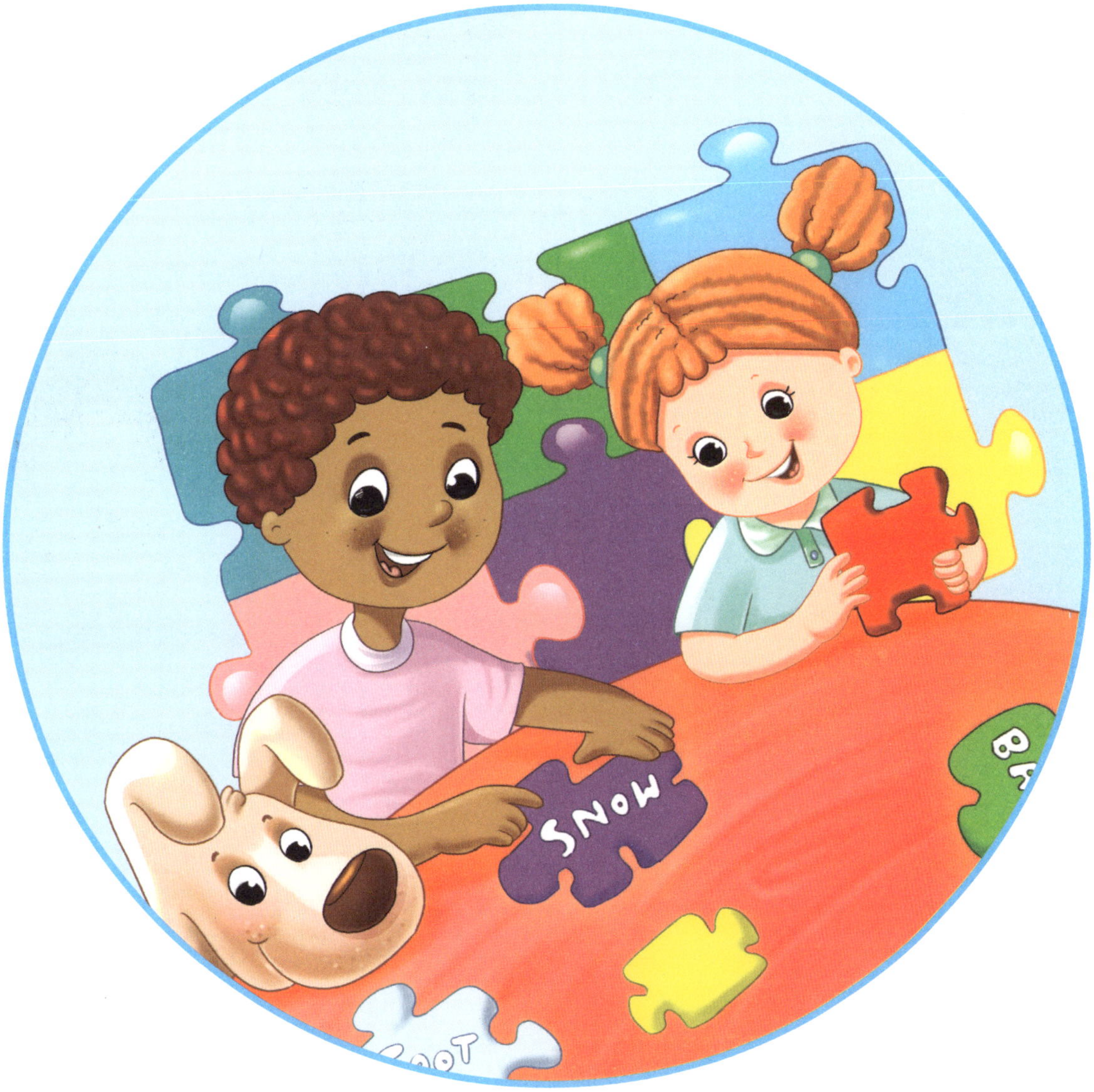

Om KIDZ

An imprint of Om Books International

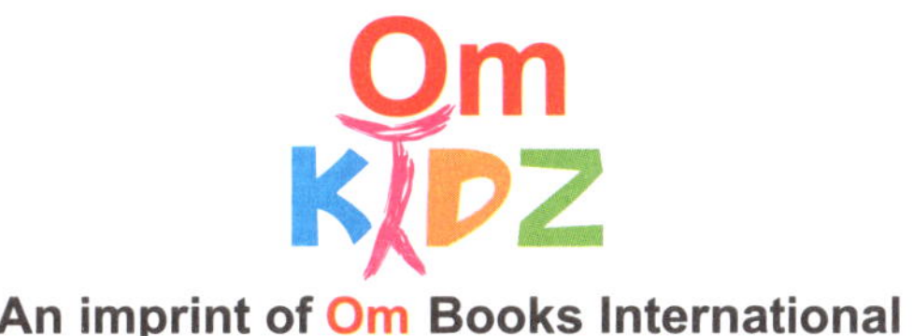

Alphabetical Order

Alphabetical order is a way to sort a list. It is done by following the usual order of letters in an **alphabet**.

bus, engine, airplane, helicopter, car

↓

airplane, bus, car, engine, helicopter

Alphabetical order makes it easier to find a name or a title in the list.

Rewrite each word list in ABC order

1. ______________________________

2. ______________________________

3. ______________________________

4. ______________________________

Alphabetical Order

Find the words in the word search below. Then write the words in the alphabetical order.

B	I	R	T	H	D	A	Y
J	O	L	G	I	F	T	S
F	R	O	S	T	I	N	G
K	T	L	H	A	P	P	Y
L	H	L	O	C	A	K	E
M	W	I	S	H	R	O	A
N	J	P	E	I	T	K	A
O	M	O	F	D	Y	R	V
P	I	P	C	F	E	W	D
I	C	E	C	R	E	A	M

happy birthday wish ice cream cake gifts frosting lollipops party

1. ______________ 2. ______________ 3. ______________

4. ______________ 5. ______________ 6. ______________

7. ______________ 8. ______________ 9. ______________

Sorting Words

Write the words under the right categories.

pasta	**milk**	**eggs**	**tea**	**cornflakes**
patty	**coffee**	**cheese**	**water**	**toast**
noodles	**almonds**	**butter**	**kiwi**	**bread**

In which list will you add ice?

Sort the Words into Different Categories

Read the words and sort them according to their categories. Write them under the right categories.

eyebrows, short, market, shoes, tall, grandmother, nose, bank, zoo, jacket, cheeks, long, airport, big, lips, aunt, gloves, daughter, trousers, mother

Women in the family	Places	Things you wear	Parts of your face	Size words

Add one word of your choice each to the list on this page.

Words That Go Together

In each tile, colour three words that go together. Find the words across, down and even diagonally.

book	rain	light
cars	magazine	sun
clock	chair	newspaper

bird	goat	squirrel
grass	ladybug	orange
pillow	quilt	blanket

vast	sick	squid
huge	happy	octopus
giant	healthy	drawers

drill	grandma	cucumber
square	eggplant	sea
spinach	wise	sleep

woods	cookies	twelve
sky	mountain	forest
sausage	tomato	trousers

lake	pond	stream
indigo	pink	poppy
bark	branch	nest

Odd One Out

In each group, find the word that is not like the others. Circle it.

1. pills, doctor, hospital, secretary, nurse

2. aunt, sister, mother, uncle, niece

3. shoe, skirt, shirt, suit, smart

4. Thursday, November, December, May, April

5. good, nice, friendly, kind, tawny

6. beak, wings, ducklings, claws, feathers

Words with Related Meanings

Put a (✓) on the correct word.

1. Which two words name things you drink from?

   glass cup plate

2. Which two words name things you do with your eyes?

   watch see tell

3. Which two words name things you do with money?

   pay sell buy

4. Which two words name ways to make art?

   draw paint cut

5. Which two words tell you that something is not old?

   young ancient new

6. Which two words tell you how sure you are?

   know guess sure

7. Which two words name bad feelings?

   cross jolly angry

Difference Between Related Words

Circle the correct option for each question below.

1. Which one of these is inside?

   the ground the floor

2. Which belongs to you?

   a pet an animal

3. Which is faster?

   stroll run

4. Which of these is younger?

   calf cow

5. Which is bigger?

   a jump a leap

6. Which is more sudden?

   pulling yanking

7. Which is stronger?

   a wind a breeze

8. Which is later?

   in the evening at night

Synonyms

A synonym is a word that has nearly the same meaning as another word.

For example: tiny-wee

Match the words to their synonyms.

1. cry	hot
2. silent	hard
3. warm	fast
4. far	weep
5. difficult	correct
6. start	wealthy
7. alone	quiet
8. true	begin
9. quick	lonely
10. rich	distant

Synonyms

Choose the correct word and write the synonym for the words given below.

large	yell	noisy	sugary	gift	talk

speak ________________

big ________________

present ________________

shout ________________

loud ________________

sweet ________________

Synonyms

Using the across and down clues, write the matching words in the crossword below.

Across

4. commented
5. loaf
8. rock
9. shortly

Down

1 task
2. donate
3 record
6 grade
7 rush
8 stain

a. list	b. chores	c. rank	d. give	e. spot
f. bread	g. stone	h. soon	i. dash	j. said

Antonyms

An antonym is a word that is opposite in meaning to another word.

For example: new-old

Choose the word that has the opposite meaning of the first word in each set.

1. quiet	noisy	silent
2. tidiness	clean	mess
3. loose	tight	fixed
4. shallow	wet	deep
5. deny	take	accept
6. none	every	zero
7. shrink	narrow	grow
8. polite	rude	generous

Write as many antonyms as you can for the word, big. How many did you find?

Antonyms

Choose the best antonym for the following words and show Kate the way to reach the cottage and hide.
break
seek
weak
win
remove
leave
exit
Hide
Reach
Lose
Repair
Enter
Add
Strong

Antonyms

foolish	difficult
sour	lost
never	new
disagreed	dislike
common	found

Write the antonym of the underlined words.

1. I have found my favourite toy. ____________
2. The test was easy for me. ____________
3. Jane always does her work on time. ____________
4. Mother likes some hot water with lemon. ____________
5. Roger's team won the soccer match. ____________
6. The farmer picked some sweet apples from the orchard. ____________
7. We all agreed with our new captain. ____________
8. The teacher showed us picture of rare animals. ____________
9. Eddie was wise to jump into the cool pool. ____________
10. Let us decorate the class with old ribbons. ____________

Compound Word

A compound word is a new word formed by putting two words together.

For example: back + pack = backpack

Circle the two words each compound word is made of.

newspaper	lunchbox
airplane	pancake
blueberry	bathrobe
pancake	armchair
thunderstorm	watermelon

Add a word to each of these words below to make a compound word of your own.

1. cow + ________ = ________________
2. honey + ________ = ________________
3. pen + ________ = ________________
4. sea + ________ = ________________
5. sun + ________ = ________________

Compound Word

Make compound words. Number the puzzle pieces on the right to match the pieces on the left.

Compound Word

Complete the compound words in each sentence.

1. We use a ____________ **pick** to pick at food stuck in a tooth.
2. I made a new ____________ **house** for my dog.
3. Aunt Polly is making ____________ **cakes** for us.
4. I saw a ____________ **boy** ride the horse home.
5. The heavy rain ____________ **thing** wet.
6. The dog chased the cat to the ____________ **yard**.
7. Kate has a healthy ____________ **fast** every morning.
8. My little brother likes to play in the ____________ **box**.
9. The baker dressed the pizza with ham and ____________ **apple**.
10. Drop the letters in the ____________ **box**.

Prefix and Suffix

Prefix

A prefix is a word part placed at the beginning of a word. It changes the meaning of a word.

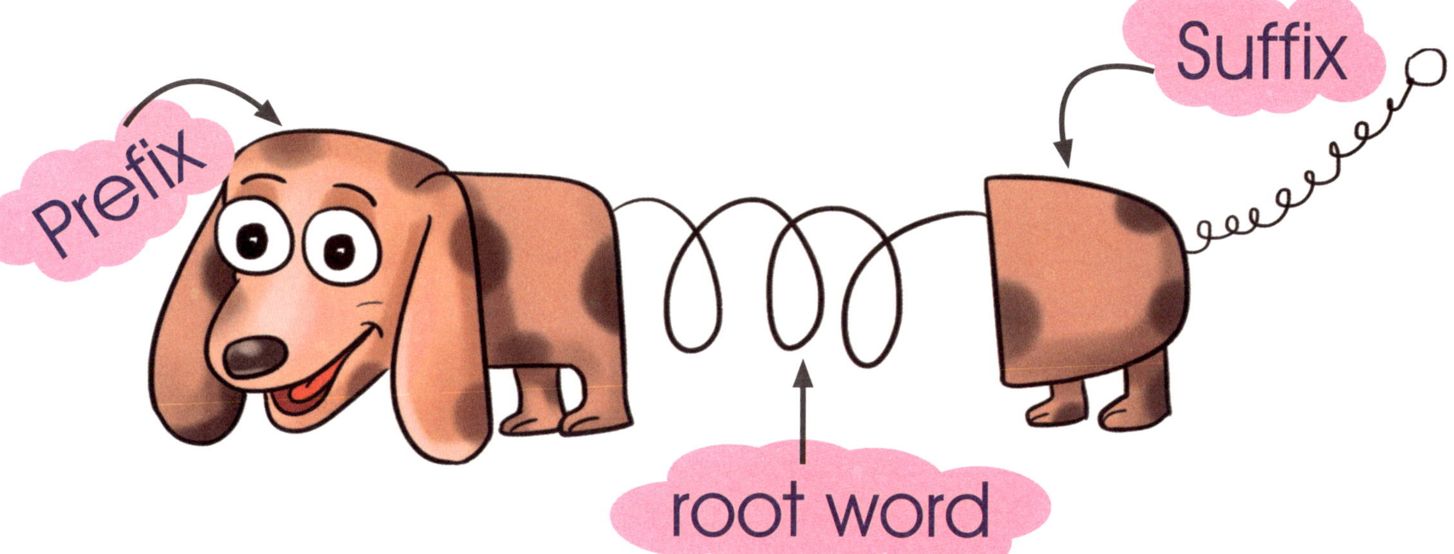

Read the common prefixes, their meanings and and words as examples.

Prefix	Meaning	Example
dis	NOT	dishonest - not honest
un	NOT	unhappy - not happy
mis	NOT	misplaced - not in right place
im	NOT	improper - not proper
in	NOT	inactive - not active
re	do again	refill - fill again
pre	before	premade - made before
de	from	derail - go from the rail
bi	two	bisect - separated into two

Prefix and Suffix

Choose and add a suitable prefix to the given words to make new words.

Prefix and Suffix

Add one of the prefixes to the words and complete the sentences.

un	re	pre	mis	dis

1. Grandma told me to wait till my birthday to ________ **wrap** the gifts.

2. The baker had to ________ **heat** the oven before he could put the cookies in.

3. Linda forgot her backpack and had to ________ **turn** home to get it.

4. Ashley was sad because she was ________ **able** to get tickets for the magic show.

5. I was about to fall as my shoelaces were ________ **tied**.

6. Imme had to ________ **do** the math problems.

7. Be careful not to ________ **spell** the words on the poster.

8. Sharon was being ________ **honest** when she did not tell the truth.

Suffixes

A suffix is a word part placed at the end of a word. It changes the meaning of a word.

Here are some common suffixes, their meaning and an example.

Suffix	Meaning	Example
-ful	full of	hopeful
-ist	person who is	artist
-ly	in a _ way	slowly
-ion	act of/ condition of being	protection
-less	without	helpless
-ible	can be	collectible
-ness	being	sickness
-able	can be	washable
-er/-or	one who	trainer/protector
-ish	having the quality of	childish
-dom	place or state of being	freedom

More Suffixes

Pick and add a suffix to each root word to make new words.

1. most – ______________
2. beauty – ______________
3. tour – ______________
4. cold – ______________
5. move – ______________
6. late – ______________
7. drive – ______________

-ful
-ist
-ly
-ment
-er
-est
-able

Circle the word that contains a suffix in each sentence below.

1. The team was hopeful to win the match.
2. The students of our class have a lot of unity.
3. Sam was very careless when running in the rain.
4. If you don't eat proper food, it will cause weakness.
5. Please don't throw that bag. It can be useful.
6. Mom bought a new gift for me that is portable.
7. The sunrise we saw over the mountains was really beautiful.
8. The warmest time of the year is best for growing these plants.
9. Many plants become droopy if you don't water them well.
10. The old man had a lot of wisdom.

Squirrels Serving

Use a prefix or suffix from the list to form a word for each meaning. Write each word in the puzzle.

1. write again
2. read wrongly
3. without care
4. able to agree
5. being kind
6. opposite of appear
7. use wrongly
8. not covered
9. state of being sick
10. opposite of honest
11. not fair
12. full of help

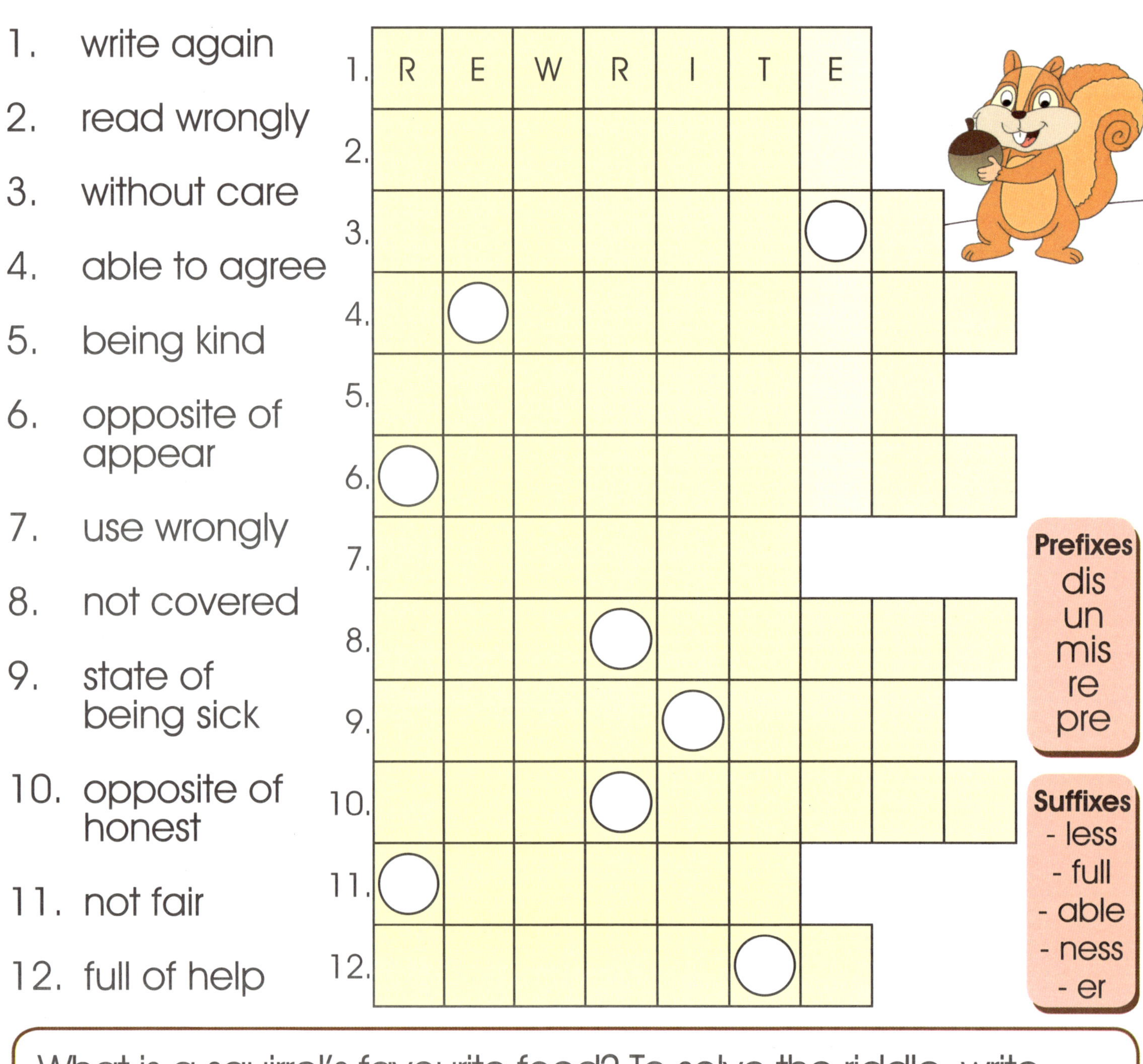

What is a squirrel's favourite food? To solve the riddle, write each circled letter from above on the matching number below.

___ ___ ___ ___ ___ ___ ___ ___ ___

7 11 18 5 15 12 17 1 3

Homophones

SAME sounds

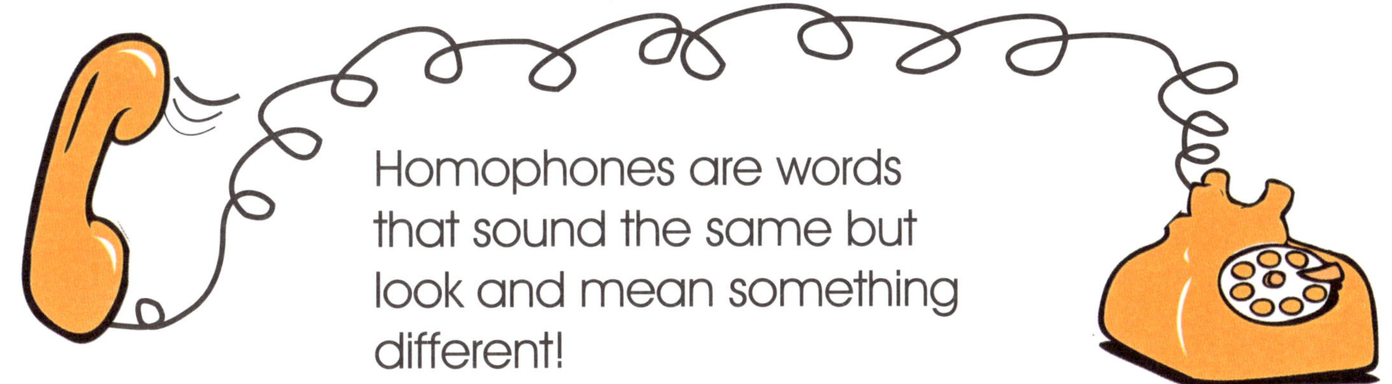

Homophones are words that sound the same but look and mean something different!

Let us read some examples.

mail	 male	 wail	 whale
 sea	 see	 world	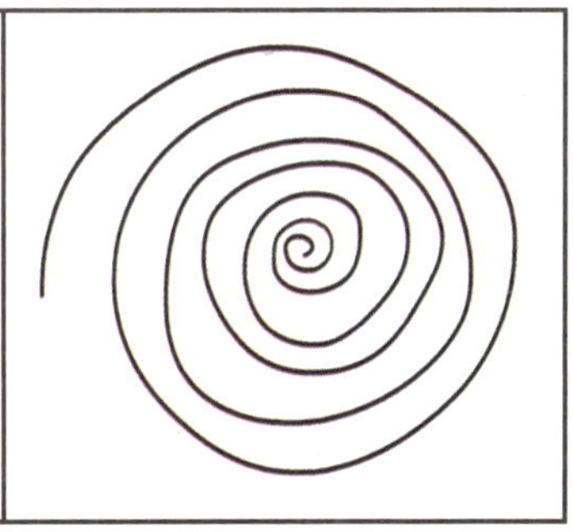 whirled
 pair	 pear	 ring	 wring

Drawing Homophones

Look at the picture and write a word for it. Now write its homophone and draw its picture.

Right

______

______

______

______

Writing Homophones

Write a homophone for each word given below.

1. be – ________________
2. break – ________________
3. i – ________________
4. knot – ________________
5. main – ________________
6. ate – ________________
7. dew – ________________
8. no – ________________
9. blew – ________________
10. hair – ________________
11. week – ________________
12. some – ________________
13. roll – ________________
14. pain – ________________
15. right – ________________

Think of two homophones of the word sent. Then write sentences to show the difference between the three words.

Writing Correct Homophones

Choose the correct word to complete the sentence.

1. Last Monday, I ____________ (road, rode) a pony along the trail in the mountains.
2. My dog hurt its ____________ (paws, pause) from digging in the yard.
3. My sister ____________ (passed, past) her time by reading stories.
4. My father cut the ____________ (bored, board) in half to build a tree house.
5. We ____________ (one, won) all the matches this year.

Make sentences with these pairs of homophones.

1. scene - seen

____

____

2. tail - tale

____

____

3. stair - stare

____

____

Homographs

Homographs are words that share the same spelling, regardless of how they are pronounced. Let us read some homographs.

bat

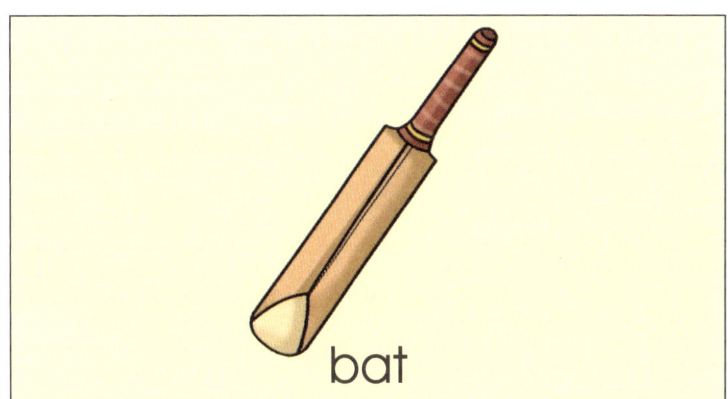
bat

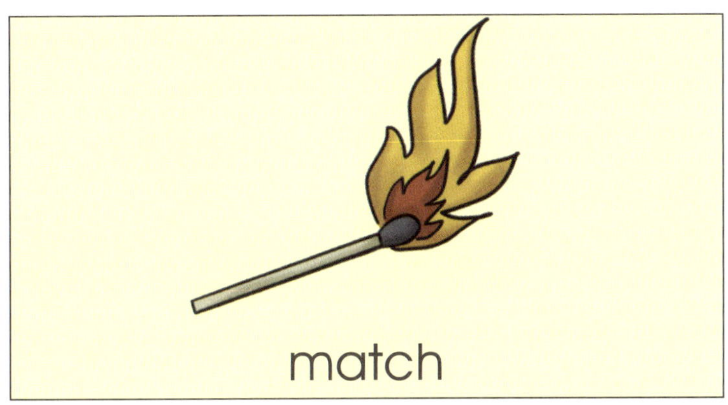
match

match

bank

bank

bow

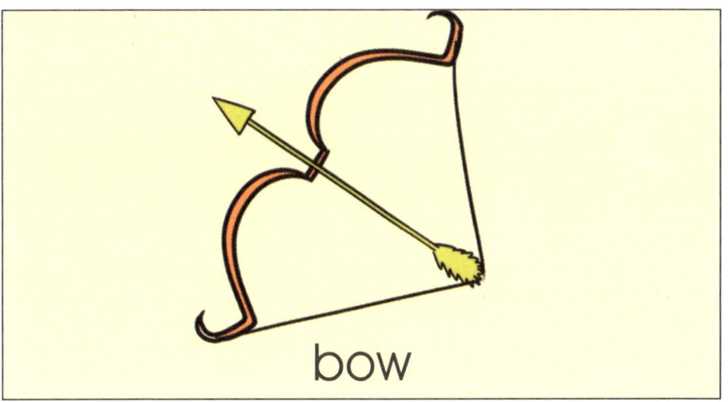
bow

Homographs

Use each word given below in sentences to show two different meanings it has. One has been done for you.

1. park - Dad parks his car in the garage.
   The children are playing in the park.
2. saw - ____________________
   ____
3. tie - ____________________
   ____
4. watch - ____________________
   ____
5. row - ____________________
   ____

Answer Key

Page 2

1. hop, mop, pop, top
2. bench, flower, grass, tree
3. cap, jacket, shoes, trousers
4. bread, cupcake, pastry

Page 3

B	I	R	T	H	D	A	Y
J	O	L	G	I	F	T	S
F	R	O	S	T	I	N	G
K	T	L	H	A	P	P	Y
L	H	L	O	C	A	K	E
M	W	I	S	H	R	O	A
N	J	P	E	I	T	K	A
O	M	O	F	D	Y	R	V
P	I	P	C	F	E	W	D
I	C	E	C	R	E	A	M

Alphabetical order of the words:
birthday, cake, frosting , gifts,
happy, ice cream, lollipop,
party, wish

Page 4

Food - pasta, eggs, cornflakes,
patty, cheese, toast, noodles,
butter, almonds, kiwi, bread,
Drinks - milk, tea, coffee, water

Page 5

Women in the family	Places	Things you wear	Parts of your face	Size words
grandmother	market	shoes	eyebrows	short
aunt	bank	jacket	nose	tall
daughter	zoo	gloves	lips	big
mother	airport	trousers	cheeks	long

Page 6

book	rain	light
cars	magazine	sun
clock	chair	newspaper
vast	sick	squid
huge	happy	octopus
giant	healthy	drawers
woods	cookies	twelve
sky	mountain	forest
sausage	tomato	trousers

bird	goat	squirrel
grass	ladybug	orange
pillow	quilt	blanket
drill	grandma	cucumber
square	eggplant	sea
spinach	wise	sleep
lake	pond	stream
Indigo	pink	poppy
bark	branch	nest

Page 7

Odd one out in each group is:

1. secretary
2. uncle
3. smart
4. Thursday
5. tawny
6. ducklings

Page 8

1. glass, cup
2. watch, see
3. pay, buy
4. draw, paint
5. young, new
6. know, sure
7. cross, angry

Page 9

1. the floor
2. a pet
3. run
4. calf
5. a jump
6. yanking
7. a wind
8. at night

Page 10

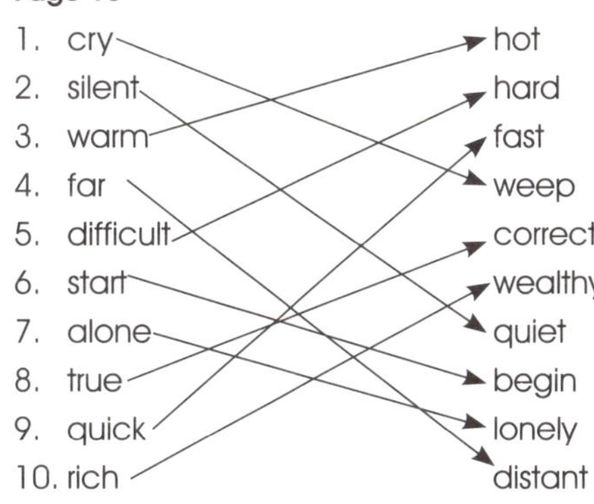

Page 11

speak- talk
big- large
present- gift
shout- yell
loud- noisy
sweet- sugary

Page 12

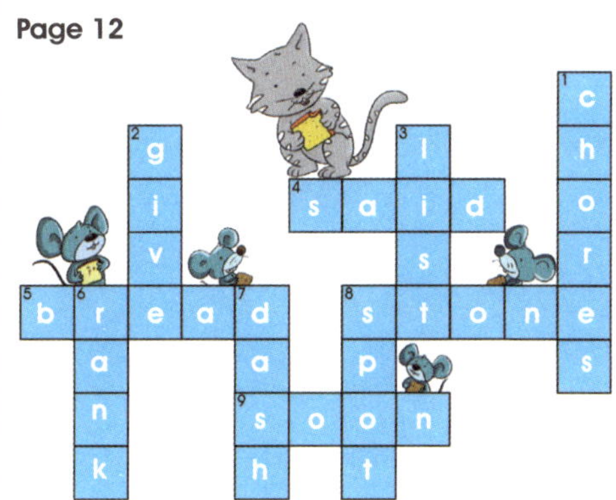

Page 13

1. quiet- noisy
2. tidiness- mess
3. loose-tight
4. shallow- deep
5. deny- accept
6. none-every
7. shrink- grow
8. polite- rude

Page 14

hide- seek
reach-leave
lose-win
repair- break
enter-exit
add- remove
strong- weak

Page 15

1. lost
2. difficult
3. never
4. dislikes
5. lost
6. sour
7. disagreed
8. common
9. foolish
10. new

Page 16

news, paper
lunch, box
air, plane
pan, cake
blue, berry
bath, robe
key, board
arm, chair
thunder, storm
water, melon
Children to make new words on their own.

Page 17

Answer Key

Page 18

1. toothpick
2. doghouse
3. cupcakes
4. cowboy
5. everything
6. backyard
7. breakfast
8. playground
9. pineapple
10. mailbox

Page 20

Children will do on their own.

Page 21

1. unwrap
2. preheat
3. return
4. unable
5. untied
6. redo
7. misspell
8. dishonest

Page 23

First exercise

1. mostly
2. beautifully
3. tourist
4. coldest
5. movable
6. lately
7. driver

Second exercise

1. hopeful
2. unity
3. careless
4. weakness
5. useful
6. portable
7. beautiful
8. warmest
9. droopy
10. wisdom

Page 24

1. rewrite
2. misread
3. careless
4. agreeable
5. kindness
6. disappear
7. misuse
8. uncovered
9. sickness
10. dishonest
11. unfair
12. helpful

Page 26

right-write
piece-peace
night-knight
ate-eight
which-witch

Page 27

be - bee
break - brake
I – eye
knot- not
main - mane
ate - eight
dew - due
no- know
blew- blue
hair- hare
week- weak
some- sum
roll- role
pain- pane
right- write

Page 28

1. rode
2. paws
3. passed
4. board
5. won

Children will make sentences on their own.

Page 30

Children owill do on their own.